The Very First Right is....

Christopher J. Barnhill

WestBow Press books may be ordered through booksellers or by contacting:

WestBow Press
A Division of Thomas Nelson & Zondervan
1663 Liberty Drive
Bloomington, IN 47403
www.westbowpress.com
844-714-3454

Scripture taken from the King James Version of the Bible.

ISBN: 978-1-4908-9179-8 (sc)
ISBN: 978-1-5127-8064-2 (e)

Print information available on the last page.

WestBow Press rev. date: 02/04/2022

WestBow
PRESS®
A DIVISION OF THOMAS NELSON
& ZONDERVAN

Contents

"We hold these truths to be self-evident, that all men are created equal, that they are endowed by their Creator with certain unalienable Rights, that among these are Life, Liberty and the pursuit of Happiness. — That to secure these rights, Governments are instituted among Men, deriving their just powers from the consent of the governed, — That whenever any Form of Government becomes destructive of these ends, it is the Right of the People to alter or to abolish it, and to institute new Government, laying its foundation on such principles and organizing its powers in such form, as to them shall seem most likely to effect their Safety and Happiness."

-The Declaration of Independence-

Introduction

Before there was a United States Constitution or even a United States of America our founding fathers met and worked on the foundation of this nation. They realized just like building a house that in the building of a nation the most important part would be laying out a solid, concrete foundation. It was time for Colonial America to turn the page on history and create a new government. The writing of what I believe to be the most important document in American History, The Declaration of Independence, was the first step in the turning of pages in the birth of this nation.

The founders believed that the people were created by our Creator with certain unalienable rights. The word unalienable is an adjective used to describe something that is incapable of being repudiated. The right to life, liberty and the pursuit of happiness were the unalienable rights that our founders laid out for the foundation of our country. William Jennings Bryan said, "the chief duty of government, in so far as they are coercive, is to restrain those who would interfere with the inalienable rights of the individual, among which are the right to life, the right to liberty, the right to the pursuit of happiness and the right to worship God according to the dictates of one's conscience." Unfortunately, the government has repudiated the rights to life, liberty, and the pursuit of happiness throughout the course of our nation.

I
The Pursuit of Happiness

A person that is in pursuit of a certain desire is following or chasing that desire in order to obtain or capture it. Happiness is a state of contentment, joy, and satisfaction.

"For God giveth to a man that is good in his sight wisdom, and knowledge, and joy." Ecclesiastes 2:26

The right to the pursuit of happiness is a right that must be controlled within the boundaries of legality to ensure that all people have the chance to pursue happiness. If there were no anti-trust laws then only the rich would be allowed to compete in the financial market. If there were no laws and punishments for murder, a man could take the life of another man for his own happiness. These are two prime examples to show why the pursuit of happiness needs legal limits.

The American dream is a coined phrase in American society that I believe to be the true meaning to the pursuit of happiness. In a person's pursuit of the American dream, they are allowed to be born in one level of society and work their way to the top level of society. You can be raised in one of the worst areas in America and build your way up to the nicest area in America. A person is allowed to choose their education and career path; you control your own destiny in your pursuit of happiness.

The right to the pursuit of happiness was repudiated by unjust boundaries set up by the government throughout the history of our nation. These boundaries were set along the lines of ethnicity and gender. Before equal rights, women and ethnic groups found restraints socially, educationally, and economically.

Women and ethnic groups were limited to where they could pursue their education, jobs they could work, voting rights, and the right to own property. Ethnic groups were limited in their means of transportation, restaurants of which they could eat and water fountains of which they could drink. These boundaries would eventually be torn down from our society through legislation and court decisions.

The fight for the right to pursue happiness shows how powerful this right is. These people stayed in pursuit for this right until they were given access to it. Men and women marched, boycotted, protested for the right to pursue happiness. They were mocked, spat on, sprayed with fire hydrants, and some even died in the pursuit of happiness, however they never quit fighting for it. When a police officer is in pursuit of a suspect, he chases that suspect until they are captured.

The police officer might get tired and may face obstacles, but does not quit until the pursuit ends in the captivation of the suspect. May it be in our life that we do not quit until we obtain and capture our happiness, our American dream.

My faith leads me to believe that true happiness and joy is found by those who strive to please God. You can pursue happiness in the possessions that the world has to offer, but true joy will only be found in your service to God.

II
Liberty

The right to liberty was not enjoyed by every person until Congress abolished slavery. Liberty is the state of a free person allowing them to be exempt from being owned by another person. Our founding fathers declared that all men were created equal and free by our Creator. The institution of slavery was a system instituted by our government that would repudiate the unalienable right to liberty. By being denied the right to liberty, slaves were also denied the right to pursuit happiness.

Imagine yourself as a prisoner in a prison cell for the rest of your life. You, as a prisoner, are a slave to the consequences of your actions and decisions. You are bound by your chains and shackles, confined to the walls and restraints of that prison. You have forfeited all of your freedom and right to the pursuit of happiness. You lost the right to decide where you will live, where you will travel, and what your occupation will be.

The institution of slavery gave a slave similar circumstances as a prisoner in prison. Now imagine, a slave walking off their master's property. The master notices the slave's actions and asks the slave, "Where are you going?" The slave replies, "I am going to pursue happiness!" How well do you think that would go? It would go just about the same way as if the prisoner tried to escape from prison and got caught.

Since the government has granted the right to liberty to every American citizen born in the United States, people have been self imposing bondage on themselves that has taken away their liberty. People have found bondage through alcohol addictions, drug addictions, gambling habits, financial decisions, pornography addictions, and abusive relationships.

"Stand fast therefore in the liberty wherewith Christ hath made us free, and be not entangled again with the yoke of bondage." Galatians 5:1

I believe that our founders listed the right to liberty before the right to the pursuit of happiness because they realized that liberty must be obtained before a person could pursue happiness. Happiness would be hard to obtain if you worked and never received a paycheck or were told where to live. Liberty is an absolute necessity to pursue happiness, and life is an absolute must to obtain liberty.

I encourage you to keep away from bondage of the flesh. If you are in bondage to the flesh, I pray that you will take that bondage to Christ and beseech Him to free you.

III
Life

"Lo, children are an heritage of the LORD: and the fruit of the womb is his reward."

Psalms 127:3

The 1913 Webster's Dictionary lists different meanings for the word life. The definition that will be forever in my mind is: the potential or animating principle, also, the period of duration, or anything that is conceived of as resembling a natural organism in structure or function.

The very first right given to us is the right to life. It is the core principal of our foundation. Just as our other two rights; this right has been limited by our government.

I believe the founders of this nation purposely listed the right to life before the other two rights. They knew that life must be granted in order to obtain liberty and then pursue happiness. If you take away the right to life, you also take away the other rights. They simply do not exist without the right to life. One must live to be free and must be free to live. One must live to pursue happiness and must pursue happiness to live life at its fullest.

The most recent attack on our unalienable rights by our government is the attack on the right to life. As long as abortion is legal in this nation, the right to life is not guaranteed. When a life is terminated in a mother's womb it then becomes a domino effect.

The first result of taking away the right to life is it takes the right to liberty away. That unborn child instantly loses his or her right to be born a free citizen. If he or she loses that right then he or she is disqualified from the right to pursue happiness as a direct result of the elimination of life.

The largest debate about life is when life begins. If you do not believe that life starts at conception I have two questions. My first question would be when does life start? My second question is if a human is not a life at conception, how did the baby survive from conception to birth if the baby were not alive? The Bible has several scriptures talking about life inside the womb.

"And it came to pass, that, when Elisabeth heard the salutation of Mary, the babe leaped in her womb; and Elisabeth was filled with the Holy Ghost: And she spake out with a loud voice, and said, Blessed art thou among women, and blessed is the fruit of thy womb. And whence is this to me, that the mother of my Lord should come to me?

for, lo, as soon as the voice of thy salutation sounded in mine ears, the babe leaped in my womb for joy." Luke 1:41-44

This scripture from the first chapter of Luke's gospel is overwhelming evidence that the scripture stands firm on the belief that life is sacred and starts from conception. The thing that sticks out most to me in this text is the babe leaped in the womb for joy. Elisabeth's child was called a babe, not a fetus. Nowhere in the Bible will you find the word fetus. Elisabeth's child leaped for joy at the news that the Savior of the world, Jesus Christ had been conceived. In the womb, he knew that his Savior was in Mary's womb. This powerful passage of scripture shows us that the baby in Elisabeth's womb was not just alive, but well aware of the situation at hand.

An unborn child that is terminated will never get the chance to pursue an education, make career choices, have a family and place to call home. That sounds a lot like a slave. When I was a child, on career day, I remember students dressed up like firemen, professional athletes, doctors, lawyers and many other professions. They had a dream they were chasing, and that dream was able to be chased all because they were granted the very first right, the right to life.

IV
The House

Kathy L. Casper wrote an essay on, "Thoughts on Life, Liberty and the Pursuit of Happiness," and she stated, "So, the pursuit of happiness is a journey we take from within; liberty is the freedom we allow ourselves; and life is the vessel which carries both our happiness and our freedom."

The right to life, liberty and the pursuit of happiness were given to us as a foundation on which we were to build this nation. After the foundation for a house is laid out, the house is then built. If the foundation is not solid and cracks, it will be evident on the inside and outside of the house. The inalienable rights that our founders gave us were the foundation and the constitution was the house built on the foundation of life, liberty and the pursuit of happiness.

The foundation has been cracked. It is very evident in the house. When the right to life has been taken away, the rights given to man in the constitution are also taken away. I was taught that the Bill of Rights were rights that can't be taken away by the government.

The baby that was terminated will never be able to speak to exercise his or her freedom of speech, pray to exercise his or her freedom of religion, or own a gun to exercise his or her right to bare arms. The only way to fix the cracks in the walls is to fix the foundation and restore the very first right endowed upon us by our Creator, the right to life.

V
The Gift

"For the wages of sin is death; but the gift of God is eternal life through Jesus Christ our Lord." Romans 3:23

Eternal Life is the ultimate gift that person can receive during their life. It is the gift that will let you live eternally, even when your body is pronounced dead on this earth.

"Let not your heart be troubled: ye believe also in me. In my Father's house are many mansions: if it were not so, I would have told you. I go to prepare a place for you. And if I go and prepare a place for you, I will come again, and receive you unto myself; that where I am, there ye may be also." John 14:1-3

It is the gift that will free you from your chains of sin and give you the power to overcome obstacles, unfair advantages and addictions that you might encounter on your journey.

"If the Son therefore shall make you free, ye shall be free indeed." John 8:36

Eternal life is the gift that will guide you in your new direction in your pursuit of happiness.

"These things have I spoken unto you, that my joy might remain in you, and that your joy might be full." John 15:11

The gift of eternal life can only be obtained through putting your trust and faith in Jesus Christ. "Jesus saith unto him, I am the way, the truth, and the life; no man cometh unto the Father, but by me." John 14.6

I want to encourage you to accept the gift of eternal life and put your trust and faith in Jesus Christ if you are not a Christian. Through Christ, our life, our liberty and our happiness will be full.

Dedication

This writing is dedicated to my Savior, Jesus Christ and to everybody that contributed to making this possible. I want to thank Mr. Claude Gunter, Mr. and Mrs. Daniel Barnhill, Mr. and Mrs. Dan Cregan, Pastor Barry Corbett, Mrs. Linda Gassiot, Mr. Eddie Cagle, Mr. and Mrs. Josh Morris, Amanda Holbrook, the Pelliesier family, Mr. Roy Schooler, Rachel McGee, and especially my loving wife, Ashlea Elizabeth Barnhill. Thank you for your dedication and belief in the right to life.

Printed in the United States
by Baker & Taylor Publisher Services